Saving the Wilderness

JOHN MUIR

*Corinne J. Naden
and Rose Blue*

*The Millbrook Press
Brookfield, Connecticut
A Gateway Biography*

Cover photograph courtesy of The Granger Collection
Background cover photograph courtesy of Superstock

Photographs courtesy of: The Granger Collection:
pp. 4, 17 (left), 22; National Park Service: pp. 7, 8
(Tom Wilson), 25 (Cecil Stoughton), 31 (Richard Frear);
British Tourist Authority: p. 11; Wisconsin Division
of Tourism: p. 13 (top); State Historical Society of
Wisconsin: pp. 13 (bottom), 17 (right), 29; Superstock: pp. 26 (top), 34; Library of Congress: p. 26
(bottom); University of Wisconsin-Madison News &
Information Service: pp. 31 (inset), 43; The Bancroft
Library: p. 37; The Sierra Club, William E. Colby
Memorial Library, by Joseph N. LeConte, coll #1859:
p. 40 (top): Photo Researchers © Farrell Grehan:
p. 40 (bottom).

Library of Congress Cataloging-in-Publication Data

Naden, Corinne J.
John Muir, saving the wilderness / by Corinne J. Naden
and Rose Blue.

p.   cm. — (A Gateway biography)
Includes bibliographical references and index.
Summary: A biography of John Muir, early proponent of
wilderness preservation and founder of the Sierra Club.
ISBN 1-56294-110-0
1. Muir, John, 1838-1914—Juvenile literature.
2. Conservationists—United States—Biography—Juvenile
literature. 3. Naturalists—United States—Biography—
Juvenile literature. [1. Muir, John, 1838-1914.
2. Conservationists. 3. Naturalists.] I. Blue, Rose.
II. Title. III. Series.
QH31.M9N27   1992
333.7′2′092—dc20
[B]   91-18106   CIP   AC

From Rose: To Sara Jessica, my very bright and almost grown-up cousin.

From Corinne: To my young cousins, Marjorie Ann and Victoria Taylor, who can almost walk to Muir Woods.

John Muir

E*arth-Planet, Universe."* That's how John Muir, who is called the "father of our national parks," once wrote his address in a notebook. What did he mean? What was he saying about himself?

The year was 1867 John had just left his family's farm in Wisconsin. He was hiking through the southern United States. Those words in his notebook could have meant that everywhere was now his home, everywhere was now his address.

But John Muir was saying more than that about himself. He was saying that he loved the planet Earth and all its living wonders. He was saying that he felt at home anywhere in nature.

Because of John Muir, we can all enjoy many of nature's wonders today. Imagine that you are standing in the middle of Muir Woods, seventeen miles northwest of San Francisco, California. You are surrounded by gigantic redwood trees. They are so tall, you can barely see their tops. Many of them have been growing for hundreds of years. Redwood trees grow naturally only on the Pacific Coast, in Oregon and California. Thanks to John Muir, they still grow there.

Imagine visiting the Yosemite Valley of east-central California. You can see an unbelievable waterfall! It tumbles more than 2,400 feet down a mountain of rock. Famous Niagara Falls on the New York–Canadian border tumbles only 167 feet! Think of John Muir when you're staring at Yosemite Falls. Also think of him if you build a sand castle at the Cape Cod National Seashore in Massachusetts. Both Yosemite and the Cape Cod National Seashore are part of the U.S. national park system. They are saved in their natural state for everyone to enjoy—thanks in part to John Muir's work.

Muir helped to preserve many such areas around the world. He didn't just love and respect nature. He fought hard all his life to protect and conserve it. John Muir is America's best-known *conservationist.*

The word *conservation* means the careful use of the Earth's natural resources, such as water and land. Conservation means that you can enjoy the same forests your great-grandmother enjoyed. It means that your great-grandchildren can enjoy those forests, too. Conservation means taking care of redwood trees. It means not polluting rivers and

Redwoods in Muir Woods National Monument, north of San Francisco, California. The trees grow naturally from south-western Oregon to Monterey County, California.

Beautiful Yosemite Valley. Thanks to Muir's efforts, it is preserved as part of a national park.

lakes. If all the redwoods die, we can never get them back again. If rivers and lakes become badly polluted, it is difficult and costly to make them healthy again. Sometimes it can't be done at all.

Action on conservation is fairly new. Through the years, some people did warn about wasting natural resources. But few paid attention. There was lots of clean air, they thought. Pure water and rich land were easy to find. Why worry? But in the 1800s, some people in the United States *did* worry. John Muir was one of them. He and others tried to teach the American people to protect our natural resources. This is the story of our greatest conservationist, and of his fight to save the wilderness.

When *John Muir* grew up, he said his address was "Earth-Planet." But he was born in the small fishing port of Dunbar, in southeastern Scotland. On April 21, 1838, Daniel and Anne Muir had their first son, John. He was the third child in a family that grew to eight children.

Almost from the time he could walk, John loved nature. He especially loved the wilderness. He never forgot his childhood in Dunbar. "Wildness was ever sounding in our ears," he wrote. He remembered walking with his grandfather along the wild shores of the North Sea. He remembered finding six baby mice in a haystack. And he remembered reading in his school book about the vast wilderness lands of the United States. Young John dreamed of seeing America's great open spaces, teeming with wildlife.

In February 1849, his dream came true. His storekeeper father wanted to be a farmer, but land cost too much in Scotland. Daniel Muir decided to go to North America. Sons John and David and daughter Sarah went with him. John's mother and the other children would join them later. John, who was not quite eleven, was thrilled with the adventure.

Off they went on a long journey by sea and train. Daniel had heard that people from Scotland had settled in the United States, in Wisconsin. At last the Muirs arrived in the little town of Kingston, about one hundred miles from Milwaukee.

Daniel bought eighty acres of wilderness land on the edge of a small lake. At first he and the

The harbor in Dunbar, Scotland. As a young boy, Muir learned to love the wild Scottish coast.

children lived in a crude shack. Later they had a fine eight-room house. In the fall of the year, the rest of the family joined them.

Young John loved the Wisconsin wilderness. There was so much of nature around him. He was in awe of the fish-filled lake and the meadow bustling with blue jays, raccoons, and deer. The summer nights came alive with the sparkle of tiny lightning bugs. John had never seen them.

One day John and David saw their first passenger pigeons. The birds swarmed over the lake in a great gray-blue cloud. The breasts of the male pigeons were rosy red, shading to gold, emerald green, and rich crimson along the sides. John wrote in later years: "Oh, what bonnie, bonnie birds!" Alas, their beauty is gone forever. You will never see a passenger pigeon swoop down over a lake. Once so plentiful, these birds were hunted to death. Not one is alive today. The last known passenger pigeon died in a zoo in Ohio in 1914.

John Muir lived in the wilderness, but he had little time to enjoy it. His childhood was hard. Daniel Muir was a stern, strict father. Often he would use a switch to punish his sons. Yet he never

The lakes and woods of Wisconsin taught John Muir much about nature.

This rough sketch shows the Muirs' first home in Wisconsin.

opened his arms to comfort them. John's mother was loving, but his father's words were law.

As the eldest son, John took the most punishment. He also did the hardest work. He rarely went to school. Nearly sixteen hours each day, John hoed and planted and plowed. As he grew older, his bright mind longed for the education he had missed. His father allowed only one book in the house—the Bible. John began to borrow books secretly from neighbors. He was punished if his father found them. In moments stolen from sleep time, he read Shakespeare and taught himself mathematics.

The years passed in this harsh way. As a grown man, John Muir stood about five feet, nine inches tall. He was graceful, hard of muscle, and lean of build. He would remain so all his years. His blue eyes were sharp, and his hair was auburn and thick. Most of his life he wore a bushy beard. When it turned white, he looked like a wise old prophet. In many ways that is just what he was.

In 1860, John Muir was twenty-two years old. He still hadn't decided what he wanted to do. He loved the land, but he did not want to be a farmer.

He loved nature, but he had other interests as well. For a while he thought about becoming a doctor. He was also a clever inventor. Untrained and unschooled, he invented all kinds of things to make farm work easier. These included clocks, a sawmill, tools, a lamplighter, and an automatic horse feeder. He was especially pleased with his "early rising machine." It stood the sleeper right on his feet when it was time to get up from bed!

In the autumn of 1860, John took some of his inventions to the state fair in Madison, the capital city of Wisconsin. His father was very angry at his leaving. But John's inventions, especially his clocks, got a lot of attention at the fair. They were reported in many local newspapers, and John won a prize of ten dollars.

John decided to stay in Madison. The city had a university, and John longed for an education. The university grounds were the most beautiful he had ever seen. The University of Wisconsin, founded in 1848, still sits on those lovely grounds on the shore of Lake Mendota.

John Muir hadn't had much schooling. He had no money. Could he be a college student?

The answer was yes. The university was fairly new and needed students. In spite of his lack of schooling, he had a quick mind. He had also read a great deal. After taking some courses to catch up with the other students, John was admitted, in 1861. To earn money, he worked at odd jobs and did some tutoring.

John did not earn a college degree because he took only courses that interested him. He was very poor, and he had to work hard. But in his spare time he kept inventing. His room at the university turned into a showplace of weird machines that actually worked! For instance, he invented a mechanical desk. Every fifteen minutes, a book was pushed up to the top of the desk and opened for study. At the end of the time period, the book was closed automatically and dropped back into a rack. Then another book was pushed up! You can see John Muir's mechanical desk today at the State Historical Society Museum of Wisconsin, in Madison.

The townspeople thought of Muir as a genius. In many ways, however, he still looked and acted like an unschooled farm boy. His beard was so untidy that a fellow student once suggested starting

John Muir as a young man. He wore a beard for most of his adult life.

A sketch of the "student desk" that Muir invented. The machine opened a new book for study every fifteen minutes.

a fire in it. As Muir later admitted, he was very shy and "always a little lonesome."

In June 1863, John Muir left the University of Wisconsin. He had become fascinated with botany, the study of plants. But he still hadn't decided what to do with his life. He knew only that he longed to explore the wilderness. His love of nature was stronger than ever.

Muir traveled north into Canada. He worked at odd jobs and explored the woods around him. He collected and studied plants to his heart's content. The more he saw of nature, the more he wanted to explore.

Muir decided to save up money so that he could take longer trips in the wild. He took a job at a broom and rake factory. There he invented new machines and improved others. In return, he was promised a share of the profits. But the factory burned down before any profits were made.

In 1866 Muir went to Indianapolis, Indiana. There he took a job with a carriage maker. His talent for inventing machines made him a success, and he earned more money than ever. But he rarely walked in the woods.

One day, when Muir was at work repairing a saw, the sharp point of a file slipped and struck his right eye. Within hours he was completely blind. Muir was afraid that his eyes were "closed forever on all God's beauty."

But in a month or so, his sight returned. The accident changed Muir's life. It made him think about what he really wanted to do. He cared most about nature. So, at the age of twenty-nine, he said good-bye to his machines and to city life. He chose instead the wilderness.

Muir decided to walk one thousand miles to the Gulf of Mexico. He would study the land and plants of the southern United States. Then he would take a boat to South America, where he would explore the Amazon River. Muir figured that his journey would take about three years.

First, he went to say good-bye to his family. His last visit to the farm went badly. Daniel Muir said that John's trip south would be "walking with the devil." Father and son never solved their differences. Only in 1885, when Daniel lay dying, did John see his father again. John's mother died eleven years later.

It was late in the summer of 1867 when Muir set out on his own. Somewhere in the Cumberland Mountains of Kentucky, he wrote his address in his travel notebook as "Earth-Planet, Universe." His trip did not take three years, and he did not reach South America. But he did get to Florida, traveling mostly on foot, sometimes by boat. He studied plants and rocks. And he came down with the fever known as malaria. It took him two months to regain his health. During his travels, Muir wrote in his notebook. His story of that journey, *A Thousand-Mile Walk to the Gulf,* was published after his death.

That walk to the Gulf of Mexico was the start of Muir's work as a conservationist. He had always been taught that the Earth was made for humans. Now he began to see that this was false. Nature did not make plants and animals to make people happy. Nature made plants and animals for themselves. Each living thing had a right to its own life. Each had its own place in the world.

In January 1868, Muir sailed to Cuba. He spent about a month walking the shores there. Still weak from malaria, he gave up the idea of going to South America. He sailed north to New York instead. From there, he boarded a ship bound for California. Perhaps there he could regain his health. And he had heard about the many natural wonders in California.

Muir reached San Francisco in March and began walking toward the mountains. He grew healthy once again, his body lean and wiry as before.

John Muir spent the next few years exploring California and the West. He gloried in the beauty and excitement of these untamed lands. His notebooks filled with tales of plants, birds, and animals. He became a well-known sight to ranchers, hunters, and settlers. His clothes were soiled and patched. But there was always a wildflower in his buttonhole and a gleam in his eye as he approached the next mountain crest. He was alone most of the time, and he was often lonesome. But he made friends, too. One friend gave Muir a dog, a Saint Bernard named Carlo. John and Carlo became close companions and traveled the wilderness.

In July 1869, John Muir, with Carlo at his side,

Muir fell in love with the Sierra Nevada
in California. This painting of the mountains
was done by Albert Bierstadt in 1868, the
same year that Muir arrived in California.

lived one of his greatest moments. Tramping the high mountains of east-central California, he found himself on a huge cliff. He looked down into the marvelous valley of Yosemite, now part of Yosemite National Park. Muir startled Carlo by shouting and flinging his arms into the air in pure joy.

He followed Yosemite Creek for some distance until he came upon another great sight. It was Yosemite Falls, with its 2,400-foot drop of rushing water. Muir later could not recall how long he stood there. He was awed by the beauty before him. That night he wrote in his notebook, "a most memorable day of days."

Of all the wilderness he explored, Yosemite Valley always remained his special place. In time he traveled all of it. John became an expert on these miles of wilderness. He lived in the valley for two years. As he wrote to his sister Sarah, he was "in constant view of the grandest of all the falls."

Perhaps Muir's feelings for Yosemite were best summed up in a letter to his brother David. Muir wrote: "I have not been at church a single time since leaving home. Yet this glorious valley might well be called a church." He later published many articles and books about Yosemite Valley. Muir's writings led to the creation of Yosemite National Park, in 1890.

Through the years Muir developed his own ideas about nature. He studied glaciers, which are great masses or rivers of ice. They form high in mountain valleys from the buildup of snow over great periods of time. Muir wrote that glaciers had carved out the great valleys such as Yosemite. That was not the popular belief. Scientists thought that sudden shocks, like earthquakes, were the cause. But Muir, a scientist ahead of his time, proved to be right. In fact he discovered a glacier, the Black Mountain Glacier, in Yosemite Valley.

He traveled to Mount Shasta, a 14,000-foot volcanic peak in California. He explored Alaska and climbed Mount Whitney. On one of his Alaskan trips he wrote of a little black dog named Stickeen that was traveling with his party. Muir thought the dog was a nuisance. But Stickeen followed him everywhere. One day, as they were crossing a glacier, it began to rain. Stickeen's paws bled from walking on miles of sharp ice. But he kept on going alongside Muir, who began to admire the little dog.

Yosemite Falls is actually made up of two waterfalls, the upper and lower falls.

Snow-capped Mount Shasta, in California, is a dormant (inactive) volcano.

Muir (right) in Alaska in 1899. With him is John Burroughs, a well-known naturalist and writer.

Then they came to a huge crack in the ice. The only way over the crack was across a narrow bridge of ice. Muir cut steps into the ice and crossed. But Stickeen was terrified. Muir knew that if he left the dog, it would die. So he coaxed and called. Finally, the frightened little dog scurried up the steps of ice. Muir was so happy that he cried. Later, he made Stickeen famous in a story that he wrote.

Some people called John Muir a "mountain man." They thought he was strange, a loner, odd. But his articles on plants and animals brought him respect. Two of his fans were Dr. and Mrs. John Strentzel, well-to-do ranchers and fruit growers in Martinez, just north of San Francisco. The Strentzels had a daughter named Louie Wanda. She was about nine years younger than Muir, dark-haired and gray-eyed. Louie was a talented pianist who probably could have had a concert career. Instead, when Muir met her, she was helping her father run the huge family ranch.

John Muir and Louie Strentzel were married in Martinez on April 14, 1880. He was almost forty-two; she was thirty-three. John must have thought that the wedding was a very special occasion, for he borrowed a white shirt and got a haircut.

Muir was used to wandering, to being alone. But after his marriage he vowed to settle down. John and Louie planned to raise fruit on Strentzel land. He did, indeed, do less traveling and more writing. Louie seemed to understand her husband. She agreed that while the grapes were ripening, from July to October, Muir could go on his beloved nature trips.

The Muirs' first child, Anna Wanda, was born on March 25, 1881. Known as Wanda, she quickly won her father's love. "How beautiful the world is and how beautiful is the time of the coming of our darling," he wrote. John and Louie's second and last child, Helen, was born in January 1886.

If Muir was not the most home-loving of husbands, he was a warm and caring father. Perhaps because of his own sad childhood, he fussed over his daughters. Whenever he was away, he wrote letters to his wife urging her to take extra special care of them. She would have done that anyway. Louie, too, was a loving parent.

Wanda and Helen Muir, at ages seven and two.

After ten years of growing fruit, the Muirs had earned enough money to sell the ranch. In 1890, they moved into Louie's parents' large home in Martinez. Now John could devote himself to conservation. He worked in a second-floor study, which he called his "scribble den." From there he could see the rolling hills of northern California. In this room, Muir wrote some of his most important books. There, too, he wrote more than three hundred magazine articles.

John Muir had become a family man, but nature remained his first love. He once told a visitor Martinez was a "good place during stormy weather." But, he said as he pointed to the lofty peaks of the Sierra Nevada, "up there is my home."

Muir was still a loner and a wanderer at heart. But his love of nature caused him to speak out. He saw that in many places the wilderness was being destroyed. In the Sierra Nevada, grazing sheep ate the grass and killed the plants. Timber companies cut down thousands of trees. Muir knew that something had to be done to save wilderness areas.

*The Muirs' home in Martinez
is now a national historic site.
John Muir wrote many of his
best-known books in the study,
or "scribble den," of his home.*

In 1892, Muir and others who cared about con-servation came together to form the Sierra Club. First, Robert Underwood Johnson, a California magazine editor, joined Muir on a camping trip. They talked about forming an association to de-fend the national parks. A group of New York sportsmen decided to help. Then other people joined in. On June 4, 1892, twenty-seven men met and signed the charter of the Sierra Club "to pre-serve the forest and other natural features of the Sierra Nevada." They elected Muir as the club's first president.

Today this organization is well known to nature lovers all over the world. It publishes books and fights for laws that protect the Earth's wilderness areas and natural resources.

By the late 1890s, even U.S. government offi-cials had heard of John Muir's work. They asked him to help a special forestry commission study the nation's woodlands. Muir loved all nature, but he loved the forests best. "The clearest way into the Universe," he wrote, "is through a forest wilder-ness." And for him the most glorious of all the world's forest trees were the sequoias of California.

There are two kinds of sequoias in North America—the coastal redwoods and the giant sequoias, also called simply the "big trees." They have needlelike leaves and bear their seeds in cones. Giant sequoias are the largest and oldest living things in the world. General Sherman is the name of a California giant sequoia that is thought to be more than 3,500 years old. It is nearly 275 feet tall, more than 100 feet around, and still growing.

Muir's great love for the sequoias helped save them. Before they were protected, these grand forests were nearly ruined by lumbermen and sheepherders. Muir was truly angry. He wrote many articles urging that the trees be saved. It took a long time, but the legislature of California finally passed laws to protect the woods.

Muir's survey for the U.S. government's forestry commission showed that many of the western woodlands were in danger of being destroyed. He was shocked at the damage and neglect. He wrote strong words about the disappearing groves, urging that forest land be set aside. In fact, President Grover Cleveland ordered that more than 21 million acres of wilderness be protected.

Giant sequoias in California. Muir's efforts helped save many of these trees from loggers and others.

The fight for conservation was far from over, however. The lumber and sheep businesses argued loudly. But the public was learning of Muir's fight. Muir wrote: "Any fool can destroy trees."

This was the time of Muir's greatest fame. All America now knew of the Man of the Mountains. He traveled to New York, to Boston, and to his boyhood home in Scotland. He wrote letters to his wife and daughters, telling them of the famous people he met.

As the twentieth century began, Muir was as tireless as ever. His untidy beard had turned white. But his step was quick and spry. So was his mind. Theodore Roosevelt was now president of the United States. In March 1903, the president planned a trip to California. He said he wanted to spend time with John Muir. Muir and Roosevelt spent three days hiking and camping in the Sierras.

Muir talked and Roosevelt listened. One thing Muir talked about was the sequoias. Said the president later about the giant trees: "I want them preserved because they are the only things of their kind in the world. . . . I ask for the preservation of other forests." He was true to his word. Roosevelt came to be known as the conservation president. He doubled the number of national parks. He preserved 145 million more acres of forest land. At Muir's urging, he named the Grand Canyon a national monument. It became a national park in 1919.

Soon after his meeting with Roosevelt, Muir took another trip. Now sixty-five years old, Muir decided to travel around the world! Off he went to Europe, Russia, India, Egypt, the South Seas, China, and Japan. He visited many famous cities. And of course he explored forests, jungles, mountains, and glaciers of all kinds.

All his life Muir had worried about the health of his daughters. In the spring of 1905 he really had something to worry about. Helen developed pneumonia, and Muir took her to the Arizona desert to recover. But it was his wife who was truly ill. John went back to California to be with her. Louie died on August 6. Muir was stunned and saddened.

Later Muir joined his daughters for a short stay in the desert. While there he discovered a forest of petrified wood that he named the Blue Forest.

President Theodore Roosevelt (left) with Muir in California in 1903. As president, Roosevelt preserved millions of acres of wilderness.

(Petrified wood is the remains of ancient trees that have changed to stone over millions of years.) President Roosevelt, urged by Muir, created the Petrified Forest National Monument in 1906. The Blue Forest was later added to it.

John Muir was now in his seventies, but he had one last great trip to make. On August 11, 1911, he sailed for South America to explore the Amazon, the Earth's "greatest river." He had just finished two books—*The Yosemite* and *The Story of My Boyhood and Youth.* In South America, Muir was given a hero's welcome, which greatly surprised him. He told a crowd that he didn't think he'd give up his present work. When asked what that was, Muir said, "Tramp. I'm seventy-four, and still good at it." From South America, Muir was off to Africa, tramping about the jungles like a youngster.

Muir returned to Martinez in the spring of 1912. Of all the wild lands that he had helped to save, he loved Yosemite best. It is a strange ending to Muir's story that, after all his many successes, he now lost his last great fight. Some say it was the one he most wanted to win. He could not save the part of Yosemite known as the Hetch Hetchy Valley.

"Hetch Hetchy" is an Indian name meaning grassy meadows. Soon after Yosemite became a national park, San Francisco asked that a dam be built on the Hetch Hetchy's river. The city badly needed water. The dam would turn the valley into a lake, which would provide more water for San Francisco.

Muir and the Sierra Club argued that it would be a crime to destroy the beautiful valley. For years they fought against it. Muir wrote articles. He made speeches. He suggested other ways to get water to the city. Still, in the end, he lost this long battle. In 1913, Congress approved the city's plan. The beautiful Hetch Hetchy Valley was soon lost forever beneath a sea of water.

Some people say John Muir never got over the loss of the Hetch Hetchy. Others say that he lost his will to live. He spent his last months working in his home at Martinez. In December 1914, he and his daughter Wanda visited Helen, who had married and was living in southern California. While there, he fell ill. He died in a Los Angeles hospital on December 24, 1914, at the age of seventy-six. On his bed were pages of a new book he was writing.

The wild Hetch Hetchy Valley as John Muir knew it. He said that its waterfalls, rock formations, and flower-filled meadows were as beautiful as a cathedral. Today, the dam that Muir opposed creates a reservoir that covers the valley.

Today *John Muir* is known as the "father of our national parks." A national park is an area that the government keeps pretty much in its natural state for people to enjoy. Muir's work and that of other conservationists laid the groundwork for the U.S. National Park Service, which was founded in 1916. It takes care of some three hundred parks and other areas, such as seashores, historic sites, and monuments, covering almost eighty million acres.

There are about 1,200 national parks in one hundred countries around the world today. The oldest, opened in 1872, is Yellowstone National Park in the United States. It covers more than two million acres in Idaho, Montana, and Wyoming. It has the Rocky Mountains, breathtaking scenery, and a famous geyser named Old Faithful. For centuries, Old Faithful has been shooting its spray high into the air about every sixty-six minutes.

John Muir was a scientist. He studied and understood nature. He was also a reasonable man. He knew that human beings needed the Earth's natural resources. He knew that industries needed them, too. But he believed that people and industry and nature could live together. He believed that conservation, the careful use of the Earth's resources, could help everyone.

Muir knew that the fight for conservation would not end with the naming of national forests. He knew that people would have to fight for their world every day, just as he had.

We are still trying to teach people to protect nature. We have learned that too many harmful chemicals are leaked into our air and water. We have learned that oil spills damage the shore and sea life. We have learned that when forests are cut down, rich soil is lost. Wind blows it off, and rain washes it away.

Many people today realize that for too long we have been too careless. They say we must all become conservationists. They say that ruining one part of the Earth threatens all of the Earth. A lake is polluted because a factory pours chemicals into it. The fish in the lake die. The birds and animals that used to eat the fish no longer have food. People who used to catch the fish in the lake cannot earn a living. No one can drink the water. The lake dies. Animal life dies. People move away.

Of all the wilderness areas that Muir hiked,
the Yosemite Valley remained his favorite.

As Muir often said, when he tried to get people to care about conservation, "Everything is hitched to everything else."

The house where Muir lived in Martinez is now a national historic site. Visitors to the house are shown a movie about Muir and then invited to wander about the grounds and the house. His "scribble den" is left as it was when Muir worked there, with pages strewn over the oak desk and cluttering the floor.

People who love nature can never forget John Muir. Many places that bear his name remind us of his lifelong fight. Muir Park in California celebrates his birthday, on April 21, with bagpipes and dances. He is remembered at Muir Woods National Monument amid the giant trees of northern California. He is remembered in the town of Muir, Michigan, as well as at Muir Lake in Australia and Muir Glacier in Alaska.

In these and other places around the world, bound by the beauty he left behind, his name and his work live on. For all time, he remains:

John Muir, Earth-Planet, Universe.

Important Dates

1838	April 21: John Muir born, Dunbar, Scotland.
1849	Goes to America with his father, brother, and sister; settles in Wisconsin.
1861	Enters University of Wisconsin, Madison.
1863	Travels to Canada.
1866	Nearly loses sight in accident in Indianapolis.
1867	Begins walk to the Gulf of Mexico.
1868	Sails to Cuba, then New York, and finally California.
1869	July: sees Yosemite Valley for the first time.
1870–1879	Travels extensively throughout the Northwest.
1880	April 14: marries Louie Strentzel.
1881	Daughter Anna Wanda born.
1886	Daughter Helen born.
1892	Becomes first president of Sierra Club.
1897	As an adviser to the U.S. government's forestry commission, recommends forest preservation.
1903	Meets with President Theodore Roosevelt; begins around-the-world trip.
1905	August 6: Louie dies.
1911	Begins trip to South America and Africa.
1914	December 24: dies in Los Angeles hospital.

Further Reading

Fifty Simple Things Kids Can Do to Save the Earth by John
  Java (Andrews & McMeel, 1990)
Glaciers by Lionel Bender (Watts, 1989)
John Muir, Father of Our National Parks by Charles Norman
  (Messner, 1957)
A Kid's Guide to How to Save the Planet by Billy Goodman
  (Avon, 1990)
The Long Ago Lake: A Children's Book of Nature Lore and
  Crafts by Marne Wilkins (Sierra Club, 1990)
Sequoias and Kings Canyon by Maxine McCormick (Crest-
  wood, 1988)
The Sierra Club Book of Our National Parks by Donald
  Young with Cynthia Overbeck Bix (Sierra Club, 1990)
Trash by Charlotte Wilcox (Carolrhoda, 1988)
Yellowstone by Carol Marron (Crestwood, 1988)
Yosemite by Lorraine Jolian Cazin (Crestwood, 1988)

Books by John Muir

The Mountains of California (Century, 1911)
My First Summer in the Sierra (Houghton-Mifflin, 1911)
A Thousand-Mile Walk to the Gulf (Houghton-Mifflin, 1916)

Index